Happy Father's Day Notebook: To The Best Dad Ever, Thanks For Everything
Father's Day Gift Book. Father's Day Gift Ideas for Dad. Blue Journal for Dad.
Paperback ISBN: 978-1-989733-35-6
Copyright Dunhill Clare Publishing 2020
All Rights Reserved. Cover Design by Sharon Purtill

www.ingramcontent.com/pod-product-compliance
Lightning Source LLC
Chambersburg PA
CBHW071249070526
44583CB00017B/2387